The Meter is Irregular

Volume 1

Parenting Teenage Werewolves

Roddy

1st WORLD PUBLISHING

The Meter is Irregular

Roddy

Copyright © 2013 Rodney Charles

Published by 1st World Publishing
P.O. Box 2211, Fairfield, Iowa 52556
tel: 641-209-5000 • fax: 866-440-5234
web: www.1stworldpublishing.com

First Edition

LCCN: 2013922197
ISBN: 978-1-4218-8681-7

Acknowledgments

Thanks Bugsy for being a great date
...and giving me two perfect werewolves.

Dedication

To Anya and Aman:

Masters in the art of
contemporary parenting workouts.

Preface

My children don't know it, but they inspired this work of infancy, whose goal was to share a few personal life-lessons-learned. It refused to emerge except in this form. Other than the preachy passages …apparently unavoidable … I respect it. Being this is my initiation into poetry, please forgive me everything. Like smelly cheese, I will ripen with time.

These poems were written on my cell phone.

Disclaimer

May Not Be Suitable For Grownups.

CONTENTS

Introduction

This morning
Following an unfavorable discussion with my
closest friend
I feel inclined to change

Because our lives count …and what we leave
behind is the evidence of the life we've lived

I resolve courage
Constrained by self honesty
Compelled to write it down

I am occasionally spiritless, but keen,
like bull for kine

Perhaps verse will inspire modest alteration
Serve honest legions
Heal invention, perhaps

Perhaps it will feed only me

In my imagination
Fear does not exist
I see a writer whose name is Victory

Who cloaks me with his love and shares my name

He is a scholar, a poet, a lover, a soldier, a bad-ass,
a humble god
Tell him your name
He will help you remember your legacy

3rd Planet from the Sun

A small earth
Bursting with sacred wine
Each peak and brook
Muttering consecrated names

But sleeping hearts
Hear only muddle
And tread heavily
Insulting holy valor

Pilgrimage

You told me you knew
I was a storyteller
Because I spoke of time and shapes

Stories of undersized journeys
Unforeseen swag and booty
Worth repeating

Natural choirs initiating daylight
Tree frogs and crickets singing for nightlight
Roosters and loons keeping time

The sun arches across the sky
And we follow
On our small journeys
Kneading dough, tilling soil, gathering values

Pressing forward
Like sea turtles
Thirsting water
Pilgrims all

Spare a Dollar?

When encountering tears
Avoid pity
Weeping shotgun
Will double the woe

Neighbors choose the right
To believe sting
You have no claim
To unearned grief

When you scoff
An extra course
You are misplaced
To your own

Compassion is not shame
But currency
Backed by empathy
And exploits

By what authority
Do you steal merit
From unrefined karma?

Family Born

Thirst drove me to the well of souls
Where I drank the deep sea
Sharing a karmic pulse
A novel opus

Love unaided dwells in our blood
Despair is a foreign assault
A germ, a viral contagion
Love single-handedly laughs in kindness

Is it corrupt to enclose a heart?
Hidden sacrifices withheld
Limits, margins, borders
Do fences protect or confine?

Heartache is a common pretext
Safety is a leash
Whatever else the world may bring
Your heart is yours to canon

I yearn to roam with you
Bar fences, walls or distance
Where spirits are barefoot Canadian
And hearths burn warm till dawn

A quiet mind is a natural leader
Audacity loves to sing and dance
Minds love to climb through fences
Hearts love to dupe and muse

An unlocked heart, unlocks hearts
Your heart is yours to canon
Love alone fits in your heart
Your heart is yours to canon

Thief

I pilfer poems
From the alter of dusty rocks and mud

Droplets in puddles
Train whistles

Unfamiliar alleys
Transcendent neon eyes

Close-ups
Panoramas

Laughter on Sundays
Worn out jeans, rightly earned

This temple
Overwhelms me

Time without end
Overwhelms me

Sleepless
I fear missing a moment
Panting alive

When you tell me
It's time to go
I will write even faster.

Character

Stand for yourself
Do you hunger for this moment?
Invite any treasure
Worthy of cessation

Reject hesitation
No breath will be shattered
Empathy is habit forming
Stand up and others will shadow

We the People

When did we waver?
Abandon royalty
Deny our birthright
Box expansion

When did we start keeping score?
Ignored, unappreciated
Unrewarded, self doubting
Glory denied

When did we change our name?
Courageous, creative
Original, complete
Masterpiece

When did we switch?
Obstruction, unkindness
Repetition, rejection
Denial

When did opportunity knock?
Bankruptcy, bitter
Shackles, sarcasm
Fear

When the moon passes
And untamed lions are honored
Our love will shine inside and out
Nevertheless

Tour de Force

To know masterworks
Know emptiness
Void of blues and hallowed soul
Vacancy of midnight jazz
Gaps flanked by notes

Blank slate on nothing
Pang of ardor ruined
Sin exposed
Poetry naked
With unabated eagerness

Grin

I am quietly joyful
As meadows
Sensing imminent showers

I seldom smile
For camera light
Which captures my bones

Poems are medicine
Children, refreshment
Wisdom, direction

Once inheritance is restored

Who else knows?

Just don't!
Feel wretched
Self destruction
Self delusion
Thumb sucking

Steal your own money
Blame the lot
Have you forgotten
Who's driving?
Where to?

How deep is your list?
My parents, my lover
My body, my money
It's not as I want it
Deserve it, I don't

A candle, spells darkness
But contrary, unnatural
Who's watching?
Who's watching?
Who else knows your secret?

Half full, half empty
Remember your ardor
Self pity, self honor
Who's driving?
Where to?

Bootstrapped Stranger

Words are not wisdom
You know the fad
Craft no hush-hush
Or shadow self worth

Who's an expert on you?
Give a nudge or a smack
Wake up, God damn it!
A kernel hides a pending tree

Worship cannot imitate
Truth knows merely love
Gather no secrets
Your heart knows the lie

Words are not openness
Tears wash away shadows
Love cannot imitate
Your heart knows the lie

Involuntary Tomb

One day, out-of-the-blue comes
You remember the moment
Everything inspires mundane illusion
Nothing matters at all
Did it ever?

Everything taken, taken for granted
As if asleep
At best a dream, that quickly slips forgotten
Dead
The sight of God, the sound of God, the smell of God,
slips forgotten

Vast is our new measured veneration
Wailing, puking, spitting emptiness
Buried on tear-drenched soil
Clinging roots and rotted bark
Peel me a verse

Surrender safekeeping
Build an ark
Like you, I am immortal
Fearlessly,
Pare me a poet

Business Matters

In business
An unexpected colleague
Delivers momentary grief
Violently twisting house and home
To rubble and vulnerability

Entertain such losses casually
Welcome the crowd of sorrows
Washing your floors and windows
For new enchantment
And mirth

Through dark deliberation
Shame and spite
Be grateful for hungry messengers
Whose starving feast
Consumes your spoilage

Invite them in
Fill their belly
Laughing
At the great gain
Of loss

Calibrate High School

Is daybreak spontaneous?
Moment to moment
Responsibility rendered
Cause and effect

Unprompted instincts
Gathering courage
Inspired affections
Cause and effect

So many opinions
Commandments and dogmas
Bibles and gurus,
Sects, constitutions

What are mistakes?
Updated data
Pathways to insight
Gateways to freedom

Common component
Ubiquitous facet
Intuitive impulse
You tenet the day

Are errors divine?
Blindfolded infants
Gathering wisdom
Cause and effect

Moment to moment
Impulse and beating
Nature recalibrates
Hearing each thought

Who knows the future?
Not even your goddess
Forging fresh options
Cause and effect

Will drama revisited
Require a retake?
Require a rewrite?
Cause and effect

Did God make us perfect?
Replete with infection
Spyware and virus
Complete incomplete

Each nature complies
Love alters the outcome
Spontaneous impulse
You tenet each day

Family Ghosts

Don't walk away from ghosts
Dream creatures you cling to
They are like guilt, and guilt is poison
A self inflicted stamp, a brand of dishonor

The one to forgive is you

Is guilt self-anger?
Suppressed and starved of self-appreciation
A lie that severs friends and families
A judgment forged in self-recrimination

The one to forgive is you

Children err, laugh, and play on
Their lesson learned, and play on
Will guilt retard the joy of games?
Be nice to ghosts and play on

The one to forgive is you

Is guilt fear of truth exposed?
Fear of acts uncovered
A weakness, a failure, a priceless love
A fool unwilling to show it

The one to forgive is you

Have you weathered enough?
Worked too hard without play?
Will you hoot and snort a giggle
And shed your mad rucksack of shame?

The one to forgive is you

Laugh with no breath
Deep bellied like a fool
Cackle at endearing imperfections
Chuckle and chortle for a lifetime

The one to forgive is you

The shadow of guilt quickly fades
With courage, self-love and self-caring
Shake hands with yourself and be happy
And help others be kind to their ghosts

Prayer

I cannot speak
Each attempt
Failure
Words fall flat

God knows

Blue neon
Eyes wide
Breath to breath
Angels speak

God knows

Enduring moments
Hushed and silent
Wisdom gathers
I cannot speak

God knows

Spilling over
Effervescent
God knows
I cannot speak

I cannot speak

God knows
Prayers chant
Tunes and whistles
Angles hum

God knows

The Cost of Art

(11 million)

Luminous strokes
Unrestrained by self-image or malice
Purely relevant
Enduring remembrance

What's it worth
To be subsumed by inspiration?
Wholly individual
Sated with childlike pride?

Fortunes
It's worth a treasure chest of delight
A soul's ransom
A poet's silence

Words like music
Suspend breath
Electrify your skin
Liberate consecrated tears

Pay an honest price
For an honest poem
And enshrine it, well framed
On your sacred coffee counter

Present it like Mozart
Improvise like Jazz
Ogle its naked form
Dance with it when courage stirs your arousal

Pay an honest price
To an honest poet
And pay her with love
And eleven million regal endowments

Skin Cancer

In my family
No one has been sold
Or traded
Purchased or on loan

Except for money

Beauty is deep
But slavery soaks the bones
A bed of nails
Is personal penance

When it pays well

Opportunity
Is bullion
Nix trial
Veto verdict

Self-exploitation

Wherever you sleep
Nightmares may find you
But cease
When your spirit

Is paid in full

Everyone's Humming

Who's in command?
The lot keeps spinning
Who's setting the standard?
Why?

Born with a song
Gathering rapture
Gathering sorrow
Music keeps playing?

Out of tune
Out of time
The frail know no rhythm
But the band marches on

Dissonant passage
Crescendo's clarity
Composed transcendence
Aria

Who's the conductor?
Who the musicians?
The choir keeps humming
Why?

Sing with spirit
Dancing shoes tapping
Inspired a cappella
Breathing suspended

Immeasurable harmonies
Luminous soul's light
Rapturous dancers
The jute box plays on

Who is the poet?
Who the composer?
When do I pause?
When to let go?

The lot keeps on spinning
Music keeps playing
Skip a beat bursting
Play on

Halfway

I am near halfway
The sun
Warms me

Clouds come
And go
Morning is constant

Dream ride
Hold firm
Resolve each moment with courage

Thank you
Honest tears
Prayer, like pure water

Daylight and night
Faithful goddess
Love will not shine aimlessly

Every moment
My dream
Is near halfway

Adolescence

No longer a child
Not yet a woman
Autonomous
Depend on me

Now that you know
You are the ward
Gather your courage
Self-sovereignty

Picture yourself
Finish the sketch
Fight for your freedom
Bar genetics

How far will you go
Sweet creature of God
Picture yourself
Bar regrets

Wear your family like rubies
Gather memories like pearls
Assemble no loans
Be a donor

Love first, think fast
Resolve what is past
Sleep enough, not too much
Feed the owner

Know your beauty is spirit
Your spirit is God
Spend the love in your heart
Journey's over.

Do You Hallucinate?

Heaven is a child
Well nourished
Well supported
Well lived

Forged
In the certainty of love

Reality intimates ardor
Dream-cherished paradise
With wonders outside your reach
This trance is reigned by you alone

Dreams feed
Or starve creation

Dream your intimate Oasis
Cultured from Iowa pearls
Each dream
Unmasks the dreamer
This trance is reigned by you alone

Dreams feed
Or starve creation

Each dream is your cocoon
Inspired with vested wings
Each dream
Unmasks the dreamer

Each mask
Another dream

Heaven is a child
Well nourished
Well supported
Well lived

Your dream will feed creation
And starve a lesser dream

Repercussion

While probing for dignity
Where should I gaze?
Query divinity?
Process of exclusion?

What is dignity, or isn't?

I am here!
Screams the loudest voice
But the obvious
Is not always obvious

Be wary

Is God embryonic?
Omnipresence implies
Infinitude implies
Love implies

Evermore emergent

Gaze in
Gaze out
Bow to every part
Bow to love

Evermore emergent

Family Genetricies

Did God appear to us
On stained glass windows?

With unrequited formalities
No protocol required
No memorized salutes
Kneeling unrequested
No fanfared salutation
No vanity of virility

Proceeded by music
Like neon laser apparitions
Michelangelo's palette
On dubstep arias

Nothing is strange
Nothing unfamiliar
Fear nonexistent
Forever friends reunited

Amidst divinity
Waking ourselves
Wholly at home
Infinity in a kernel

How to Stay Awake

How do I christen your name?
Imploring me not to let go
Understanding is not Being
You are speaking plainly, but I fail to take note

Your accent is everywhere
Whispers and shouts
Knowing, is not Being
You are calling me plainly, but I fail to hear

Your voice is ubiquitous
Uttering my name
Wake up, wake up
Am I dozing again?

How does sleep tiptoe?
Impossible really
Wake up to each sunrise
You are visible plainly, but I fail to see?

Shall I be patient?
A moment is ageless
Intolerable waiting
Impossible absence

Oneness vacated
Detail on detail
A desert of dreams
The dreamer is absent

Breathing suspended
The poet is calling
I hear my name Victory
Firmly awake

Impossible moments
Dreams without dreamers
Parentless origins
Bless me awake

Money Buys Happiness

Earn millions, billions, trillions!
Riches buy happiness
Spent eagerly zealous
On someone in need

Product net trillions
Fortunes aid billions
Money buys happiness
Thoughtfully, set wise

Wealth culmination
Currency's nature
Financial dynamics
Wealth wishes sharing

Gather your assets
Early to rise
Care for your bones
Wealth settles your goddess

Retired

Through you, dreams are spot on
Let go of plans
Accept what waits
Enjoined

Excellent summation
Beneath the form of you
Individuality lost
Do not weep

I hear your drowning holler
Yet water is nowhere near
I feel your yearn
And admire the canyon of complexity

Concede
Shed littleness
Consume royal graces
Grant fortunes to worthy travelers

Do not sob
I am priceless now
And caring more tenderly
Than during my living

What did you see?

In the eyes of God
We are children

In the eyes of God
Death has no credo

In the eyes of God
Life has no credo

In the eyes of God
All are born sovereign

What can I live without?

Warren's 401K Advice

(Saving Account)

Today, are you meager?
Are you moneyed?
Will I feel wretched for you?
I won't debase you with my pity
You sovereign your assets

Inside mediocrity, nature triumphs
Or discolors
Inside opulence, nature triumphs
Or discolors
Will you sovereign your assets?

Are we born kings and queens?
Monarchs among the homeless
Rascals with power
Have you judged either?
By what authority?

At closing bell
Moral fiber is your currency
Love, your best return on investment
Bless everyone
A measure of royal legacy

Gratefulness yields a high return
Inspiration, an excellent startup
Forgiveness is the height of culture
Condescendence, personal bankruptcy
Unselfish love, a right royal endowment

Truth is always noble
Simple, always best
Love is always hopeful
Service brings you rest.

Who is Still Thinking and Why?

Why is perfect
No matter the answer
You inquire once more
Why?

Curiosity is an honest child
A lover's swollen thrill
Sustenance
Ardor with Wonder

Sincerity is intrinsically nosy
Why is magic
Without ceremony
Informal, bare foot grubby

Why
Is target practice
Mastery
Can you afford it?

My Daughter Bought a Dog

Of course you would choose happiness
Who wouldn't?
It is our right
The fortune of being human

A usual thing

Young
It is hard to comprehend
A mother and father
Cherish the eternity of every day and night

A usual thing

Is there no exception?
Wind blows cool when you say happy
Wind blows hot when sad
Love is past interpretation

A usual thing

Youth is supple
Bending easily to the winds
Eager to be firm
It betrays its nature

Unusually curious

Does love today
Disagree with yesterday?
Will youth react in old ways
Gathering new names to hide its lost recollection?

Unusually curious

Our voice is not gunshot
But ears will make it so
Our voice is bursting applause
But ears do not hear it

Unusually curious

Is youth so quick to be offended?
Be quick to think beyond offense
Each crease and crinkle upon old faces
A tour de force, God's liberty

A usual thing

Is it so hard to trust ourselves?
Is innocence betrayed?
Is love a righteous battle field?
Misjudge, consider, rebuild

My daughter bought a dog today

Virtual Parent

Sunglasses bestow superpower
Facebook heals ignorance
Virtual war is motionless murder
Virtually
What's your tally?
How long will you cooperate?

Community

How will you serve?
Righteous imitation
Duty, obligation
Overzealous culpability

Who will you serve?
Mortgage banksters
Religious opinion
Strained piety

Will this gratify you?
Enchant you?
Inspire you?
Which poet unbolts you?

Effortless service
Inspire generations
Magnetic, irresistible
Bona fide, self rewarding

Self honesty
Self love
Self worth
Self generosity

How will your serve?
Be true to yourself?
Be you
Be

Silent Witness

Is my goddess silence?
Speaking through chattering streams
Falling brown leaves, ambitious bows
Unsullied soft earth, amorous mosses

Silence
Speaking through tears
Each smile, dying breath
Each inhale of baby's feet?

Teen

Are we two worlds?
Ever-altering
Earth-quaking, war-making
Warm oceans and polar caps

New life, new death
New love, new insight
Ever altering
Expanding, collapsing

Are we two worlds?
Inhale, exhale
Man and God
Eternal, ephemeral

Are we an ocean?
Infinite droplets
Inexhaustible sunsets
Unutterable awe

Are we permanent?
Everlasting, unending
Creator, creating, creation
Being always, always morphing

Are we timeless?
Grand illusion
Self-delusion
Hallucination, mirage

What are we now?
What aren't we now?
What does it feel like
Vacuity in Iowa?

Are we perpetual
Simple, silent, omnificent?
Fear alone
Believes otherwise

Nature Serves

Change nothing
The best is yet to come
Always

Change gravity
Holding the lot together
Always

Change predictability
Irresistible
Always

Welcome change
The best is yet to come
Always

Change your seductress
Overpowering
Always

Change neutrality
Public opinion is otherwise chauvinism
Always

Change growth
Ever to the fore
Always

Change justice
Blameless affection
Always

Change sound
Thought chasing thought
Always

Change prospect
Splendid, welcoming, present
Always

Change ocean tide
In, out, ever gainful
Always

Change death
Birth
Always

Change rhythm and pulse
Inhale, exhale
Always

Change loss
Liberty of tenure
Always

Change sting and delight
Confusion and choice
Always

Change gravity and love
Omnipresent
Always

Change nothing

Biograph

Childhood
Sounds shine neon in my mind
Omniscient, omnipotent, omnipresent, infinity.
What more need I learn

Adolescent
Don't teach me what to learn
I already know curiosity
Omniscient, omnipotent, omnipresent, infinity, love,
music.

Adult
Fit in, fatiqued
Gaze and hum like one and all
Melancholy definition
Big words, big thoughts, bigger than me

Retreat
Sounds shine neon in my soul
The origin of thought, words and music
Learning perpetually

Exit
I am
What I am
No sound or word is evenly vast
Omniscient, omnipotent, omnipresent, infinity, love,
music.

Modern Theory

Simple logic
Big Bang
Energy scatters everywhere
Evolution of matter and biology
We are stardust

How old are our memories?
Allied to the origin of matter,
Energy, the primary poet
By simple logic
We are one

We vaguely sense our sovereign seed
But grovel in false promises
From need to feel our unstained garment
From need to know our hunch was right
Frustration

Each symbol hints origination
Perception implies foundation
We are wonderful
We have won
Have one

Prudence

What have you heard?
What is taught?
Conformed
Social misconception

Trust yourself
Question playfully
Gather pride
Check false authority

Love is innocent
Don't bind
Nor tether bound
By golden chains

Chose worth
Your wealth
Gather wisdom
Fool all day

Money lures
Present lost
Gather memories
Invest in you

Children's eyes
Shine effervescent
Multiply your portfolio
Its holy light

Unhealed

Ten thousand natives
Who makes you livid?
Salting your gashes?
Stretching your limits?

Who's coupled to you?
Why?

Who simmers your wits?
Heart-steels sentiment
Teeth clench, tongue Abusive
Hate

Who's coupled to you?
Why?

Gold Coins

Where you are now
Leap in and play
Initiate fun
Distinguish patterns

Intuit the rules
Amend what you can
Gather your coins
Predict aspiration

God's eyes, God's smile
Your breath, God breathes
Gather your coins
You are the goal

Silent player
Silent prayer
The screen is the game
Gather your coins

Players play,
Playing pays,
Engaging completeness
Gather your coins

Nothing Is

Is there anything left to achieve?
Someone to hear
Nowhere to go
Presumably be?

Fifty years
Tethering episodes
Surveying me
Virtually comical

Labor
Play
Dilemma
Asleep

Tender
Adoring
Throbbing
Forgotten

Surrounded by honor
Bound with defiance
Hopeful
Extinct

Naught to increase
No one to dread
Zero fragmented
Zilch

Case in Point

Be pleased
For the lot
Presently
Your future is resolved

Reap today
Attend what's at hand
Allow your age
Be candid

Avoid absence
Honor history
Predict your outlook
Be welcome

Stay warm
With memories
Celebrate sounds
With the wink of your eye

Greet love
On the spot
Be ocean waves
Inhale

Your breath
Justly priceless

Would you sell it
For gold and promise
Pony rides
And cheerleaders?

Draw in, exhale
Opportunity is freely resolved

Can you walk?

Without witnessing divinity
Can you speak?
Without witnessing divinity
Can you hear?
Without witnessing divinity
Can you love?
Without witnessing divinity
Are you alone?
With what ears do you hear
When you are dreaming?

Not Withstanding

Is love a magnet?
What force does it obey?
Ubiquitous, unstoppable, ever-growing
It has no master, it takes no mistress, and gravity is its
plaything

Wars forgotten, weapons rusted
Love lives, love grows

Close to me
A vine strangles what is not me, what is not love

Streaming downloads and drowning in tears,
Emergent pain, an upgrade
Is love time? Is love a vacuum?
Not one day is backward

Gather your guts
Fear no detour
Reverence your flaw, sense it fully
No one can resist love's tide forever.

What's Stuck in the Vault?

I treasure empathy
Over abundance
Success
Spontaneous music
Or pure art

Treasure wits
Over wise words
Lucid dreams
Long family trips
Books unwilling to end

I treasure our gaze
Above Canadian blue mountains
Sunset gold oceans
Crystal silver caverns
The Louvre

Treasure listening
Over waterfall choirs
South China thunder
Infant gurgle and mirth
Guitar virtuoso

Treasure aroma
Over meadows Tibetan
Coffee in Paris
South Indian curry
Your new morning skin

Treasure flavor
Over sinful rich ice cream
Singing unfettered above Katmandu cliffs
Speaking in tongues
Or warm licorice toffee on cold London streets

Treasure touch
Over feather and tickles
Amorous tussle
Warm breath and sweat
Balmy Caribbean moans

Treasure intuition
Over inventive inspiration
Celestial pleasure
Mystical cognition
Passing omniscience

Treasure character
Over senses
Freedom
Life force
Our next breath

Pauper Queen

Recall truth
What else is imaginary?
Legitimacy is not a wolf at your door
Fact, is not a shadow of fear

Truth will stand on its head in your favor

Recall truth
Something invented
Without fear
Envisage emptiness

Fear worn out of your soul

Are you reality?
From rapture
From ecstasy
Nowhere exists

Truth will stand on its head for your concentration

You've seen your own goddess
Distorted her name
Why hide from her whispers?
She longs for your laughter

She will stand on her head for a giggle

Dos and Don'ts

Frostbitten feelings
Don't blame the world my dear
An old fashioned, outdated habit

Will you detour for love my dear?
The world is young and delicate
And craves your appreciation

Would you keep a list of faults in a flower garden?
An old fashioned, outdated habit
Lie naked in soft mountain green, wonder the endless
blue

Bless everything that grows
Everything grows
Reprocess the rubbish, accelerate growth

Why detour from love?
Discard frozen minds
Dissolve in self adoration

Assemble your courage
Fiercely face the daylight hours
Create no scapegoat

Carry a quiet heart
Or a neon voice
Be comfortable, my dears, and unthaw freely

Least Resistance

Love is a quiet thing
Embrace, pet you softly
Until you are ready
Anticipating wonder

Love dissolves
The marching masquerade
Paraders and sidewalks
Academic conclusions

Is love a costume
An identity
A paycheck with wow?
Is it home, marble, silk and fine wood?

Love is a subtle thing
A fat empty belly
Breath softly suspended
An absence of fear

Love is doubtless
Two worlds, then one
A tempest of breath
An absence of me

Love is easy
A trial of no conflict
With whom will you wrangle?
A naked disguise?

Pesky Spouse

Be at ease, Dearest,
You are home
A self-made kingdom

The only outcome …you would wind up with me

No apartness
No absence of safety
Everyone you love beside you

As always

The manner of living
Despite the road traveled
Ends with death

It is a lie, an illusion

The ones you love came from dust
Again and again
Is it the dust you love?

The only outcome …you would wind up with me

Do you want eccentricity forever?
I hear souls who love are stitched together
Always by our side

The only outcome …you would wind up with me

Safe Bed Rails

Pardon adventure
A journey
Yet traveled
With undefined risk

Pardon boundaries
Familiar beds
Routine comforts
Safe goals and common choices

Pardon courage
Fear suspended
Faith, even a mustard seed
Leap

Pardon endurance
Confidence stolen
Progress extinguished
Tragedy refused

What champion?
Shakespeare, Einstein, Gandhi, Keller,
Cummings, Disney, Mother, Father
Is it you?

Exceptional glory
A passage endured
Secrets revealed
Audacious self-savior

Who will admire you?
Mainly your heroes
Commencement ignites
With one simple question

A Daughter is a Simple Thing

It is undemanding for me to love
It is as simple as passing gas
Nothing stands in the way
Not even denial

No deviation
No evaluation
No incurable drama
It's as simple as passing gas

Rewrite the world
Make it a poem
Melt your hidden fears
Into golden jewelry

Wear your wedding demeanor
Sparkling with royal genetricies
It is your birthright
Simple for you now

Let love be your currency
Spend it freely but wisely
Invest in humanity
Her horrors are not equal to her love

My faith is in you
I have starlight in my eyes
I do look at you, beautiful
I do look for you, beautiful

I see you
I see mother
I see father
I see brother

I see beautiful
I see love
I see brilliance
It is as simple as that

Clay Pots

Is history dust
Assembling narration
Glimpsing possibilities
Figuring generously?

Clay is not fated
Who decides?
Contour, color, size and style
Figure liberally

Dehydrated?
Dampen
Misshapen?
Build it up

Pliable, unyielding,
Soil in every pore
A hearty mess of mud
Are we assembling history?

Is fate our master?
An onlooker of death
A vigorous mess of mud
Charitable clay

History
Can we let go?
We are not fated
Who decides?

Is history pulse?
Dampen, remold
Rehydrate
Assemble narrations

Breath deep
Exhale historically

Will and Testament

(Walking South on South Main Street)

Unwrapping skies
Clouds ripping
Soul elevated
Memories encoded

Genetic inheritance
Father to family
Breathless vitality
Soul becomes Soul

Trust instinct
Never impulsive
Gather courage
Walk straight and believe

Your tools, your senses
Keep clean and well oiled
Speech is your lineage
Words destroy wars

Battle internal
Weapons are sound
Own love and be simple
Soul becomes Soul

Propaganda

More hours in the day
Overwhelmed
Didn't sleep last night

Am I ugly?

No coffee
Father never hears me
Personal preoccupations

Am I invisible?

Sacrifice everything
No one appreciates
Nothing of my own

Abandon holy cows, repetitious propaganda

With or without sleep
With or without time
With or without means

You are noble today

With or without words
With or without names

With or without viability

You are noble today

A thief desires darkness
A calf worships cows
To give, you have to earn

Who resists the natural world?

Global power is hollow
Acknowledgment wishes empathy
Reigning triumph, resist overeating

Is the world your self-image?

Choice

I love to watch musicals
And love supersedes all arguments
Assemble your muses
Inspiration melts rock
Script, music, direction, effects
Love will find you
And stride the avenues of rapture
Teach, learn, love, act, cinematography
Edit well.

Target Practice

Choose your mark respectfully
Set, aim, release
Prefer love

Archers observe targets
The target is key
Be equipped to love

Pull back, hushed, exhale, release
Practice labors skill
Love subsumes

Talent follows confidence
Poise prolongs vigor
Depth pursues love

Sans target
Pardon skill
Set, aim, convenient love

Graduate

Continually cultivating
The world enjoys a cherished child
A laughing Buddha

Is there no commencement for an honest heart?

Will a natural spirit seize its breath?
Tighten with dread or sting?
No memory, no vault unopened, no poverty

Walk off, hush, remember

Is life school?
An accepted valiant explorer?
Hearts healing hearts?

A secret ...give it plainly
To whom it deserves
Hush

Almost Stewed

Oh
Where is obscurity?
Does it subsist?
Is it outer?

Faint, slight, trivial
Is that all?
Can there be shadows
Surpassing the sun?

Nothing altered
Zero misused
Shadows are no one
Oh, I am light

All I imagine
Nothing but light
Time is a shadow
Oh, I am light

Dark Darkness

Will you stay?
Isn't love sustainable?
Impious again
Neither Eastern nor Western
Adoring all faiths
Will you stay?

Why do you taunt me?
Stealer of breath
I know your rapture
Inhaled your cosmos
Not body or soul
Won't you stay?

Elevated traceless
One constitution
Neither natural nor ethereal
Enraptured but empty
All
Stay

Still you divorce me
Denounce me
Abuse me
Why won't you reside
Vacant habitation?
Aren't you God?

Self-Service

Is pain inevitable?
Suffering a choice?

The world is a feast
Eat content or discontent
As you like

No charge
Gratis
We are family

Opportunities?
As you like
Tell your dream to the ones you love

The rules?

Enjoyment -Throbbing
Innocence - Control
Devotion - Isolation
Spring – Fall

Richness - Irrelevance
Abundance - Insufficiency
Battle - Inaction
War

The world is a feast
Limitless flavors
Spice it as you like

You will fit right in.

Worrisome

Foretold ahead
Peril is a short-circuit instinct

Worry is a blind bastard

A time traveling serpent
Faster than light speed

Now you have health
Tomorrow will I have health?

Now you have love
Tomorrow will I have love?

Now you have security
Tomorrow will I have security?

Now you have success
Tomorrow will I have success?

Now you have riches
Tomorrow will I have riches?

Today you have worries
Tomorrow will you have worries?

Foretold ahead of time
Worry is a blind bastard

Today you have today
Tomorrow will you have today?

What to Add and What to Leave Out

Can you change the past?
No
All protestation
Brought you here
Want to get somewhere?

Don't like your looks?
It's your expression
Not your nose
Past won't change
Lest you spot it clearly

The song you sing
Echoes in your own canyon
Gather sweet notes
It's your heart
Not your voice

What's the recipe?
Add chocolate chips
Past is past
Fresh from the oven
Do you bake?

Inside Your Pocket

Despondency comes
Loneliness comes
Malignancy comes

Somewhere

Laughter comes
Compassion comes
Inspiration comes

Somewhere

Where is the switch?
That turns toil
To joy
Despair
To hope
Isolation
To love

Serve others.

Empathy comes
Nobility comes
Fulfillment comes

Somewhere

Household Antidote

Who'll witness your nightmare?
When love is disabled
Family helpless
Spirit turns grey

Who'll hear your voice?
When agony rises
Murk overshadows
Disaster hits twice

Who'll know you?
During labor and birth
When your son utters Rumi
When your soul leaps complete

Who'll see your first instinct?
Awake in the morning
Asleep in the day
Weeping in pleasure and weeping in woe.

Have you bitten your nails?
Gathered grey hair?
Is everyone home?
Are your dreams ever wicked?

Who can spare anguish
Opting calamity?
Hope is your remedy
Suck out the toxin

Fret is a venomous snake

Coffee House

(Revelations)

History declares
There is only one purpose for a coffee house
World salvation

Like pilgrims, we gather and pray

The monks
Laptop equipped
Look up, undistracted

Subsumed in caffeinated worship

Booths nearby contemplate war
Those who are weak
Need protection

From the loudest voice

Thinkers, artists, entrepreneurs
Dedicated spiritualists
Shine transcendent

The ardent glow of sanctity

Rise early
Worship daily
Honor every aroma

Prefer tea

About the Author

Rodney Charles

Piles of Bones

(Saskatchewan)

My Raindrop day
When this vast prairie expanse is squeezed
Between white cotton clouds and spring green flats
Where northern winds scratch playful deafness in my
ears
Teething through royal black mud where crows and
sparrows peck

To scavenge grit and seeds still frozen from long
winter nights.
She celebrates with me here and inhales the fragrance
of my birth
Prairie gulls drift above.

Azure sky, like Brazilian marble, bends round and
under prairie
From unknown distances, perhaps forever.
Here, she celebrates me and remembers the fragrance
Of cedar and dripping branches
Of pine needle floors moist as sponge
Of roots and rotting treefall
Of dust sunlit rays piercing grey mists of cloud
Nurtured and unafraid, she celebrates me.